The New
Brown Bag

The Shining Light

The New
Brown Bag

The Shining Light
26 Children's Sermons
with Activities

Randy Hammer

THE
PILGRIM
PRESS
Cleveland

For Jude and Bethany Grace, with much love and affection.

SUSTAINABLE Certified Fiber
FORESTRY Sourcing
INITIATIVE
Label applies to the text stock www.sfiprogram.org

The Pilgrim Press, 700 Prospect Avenue, Cleveland, Ohio 44115, thepilgrimpress.com
© 2009 Randy Hammer

GNT designates Scripture taken from the Good News Translation, second edition,
copyright © 1992 by American Bible Society. Used by permission. NRSV designates
the New Revised Standard Version Bible, copyright © 1989 by the Division of
Christian Education of the National Council of the Churches of Christ in the U.S.A.
Used by permission.

Printed in the United States of America on acid-free paper

14 13 12 11 10   5 4 3 2

Library of Congress Cataloging-in-Publication Data

Hammer, Randy, 1955–
    The shining light : 26 children sermons with activities / Randy Hammer.
        p.   cm.
    ISBN 978-0-8298-1868-0 (alk. paper)
    1. Children's sermons. 2. Object-teaching. 3. Church year sermons. I. Title.
BV4315.H2783 2010
252'.53—dc22
                                              2009035093

Contents

Preface

This book is a continuation of the stories in my previous book, *The Singing Bowl: 26 Children Sermons with Activities*, published by The Pilgrim Press in 2009, and *The Talking Stick: 40 Children's Sermons with Activities*, published by The Pilgrim Press in 2007, although any of the books can be used independently. Many of the stories and lessons to be found in this small volume have been developed and shared with children of all ages at First Congregational Church, United Church of Christ, of Albany, New York, and the United Church of Oak Ridge, Tennessee. There are stories and lessons that are particularly appropriate for special Sundays in the year, such as Palm Sunday, Easter, Pentecost, and even Super Bowl Sunday; for Sundays during the seasons of Epiphany, Lent, and Eastertide; for days when baptism or mission will be celebrated; or on Sundays near Earth Day or the end of the school year.

Generally speaking, my preference in using scripture passages with children is the Good News Translation, designated by GNT, because it is often considered particularly suitable for children. However, occasionally a different translation is preferred, most often the New Revised Standard Version. For each scriptural basis of the stories included the suggested translation is noted.

I would like to take this opportunity to thank you for joining me in this important endeavor. Special thanks to those who have utilized (and hopefully found value in) my previous children's sermons collections, *The Talking Stick* and *The Singing Bowl*. I am happy to share these new stories with all those who have a love of children and a love of bringing children and stories together for the enjoyment and betterment of all.

Introduction

Reflections on Light

Light. How appropriate that the word "light" be included in the title of my latest collection of children's sermons. Light, as a metaphor, is something that has been a growing interest of mine in recent years. I find intriguing a number of references in the Psalms. "How precious, O God, is your constant love!" the psalmist exclaims, "because of your light we see the light" (Psa. 36:7, 9 GNT). "Send your light and your truth; may they lead me . . . ," he prays in another place (Psa. 43:3). And "Your word is a lamp to guide me and a light for my path" (Psa. 110:105) we learned as children in Vacation Bible School. Light is a metaphor for truth, guidance, direction, the way one should go. I have drawn from the light imagery many times in the course of my ministry, with both children and adults.

The Society of Friends, or Quakers, most readily come to mind when I think of light imagery. They speak of "the light of God in every person." And there is a Quaker saying to the effect of "standing in the light." Perhaps my own interest in light as a metaphor was heightened when I learned a few years ago that one of my great-great-great grandfathers was "one of the first Quaker brethren to migrate from Pennsylvania to East Tennessee" (as the historical record states it), the place where I was raised and call home. But one certainly need not affiliate with the Friends or Quakers (I am affiliated with the United Church of Christ) to appreciate the beauty and wisdom to be found in light imagery.

Isn't this at least part of what we hope to accomplish in children's sermons: To uncover the light of God that is present within every child? To assist our children in standing within the light of truth? Isn't our hope to share with our children guidance, direction, the blessed way of life? Is it not to illuminate the way of what it means to be one of God's faithful children? To show what it means to be fully human and persons of respect, integrity, justice, and compassion? I reiterate, how appropriate is the title *The Shining Light.*

No greater task can we think of than that of holding "the shining light" before the children of our families and churches.

1
Going Out on a Limb
Followers of Jesus Often Take Chances

SCRIPTURE: Luke 19:1–10 GNT

OBJECT FOR SHARING: A tree limb as large as is convenient

PRESENTATION: This lesson might be shared during the season of Epiphany, drawing a connection with the magi, who "went out on a limb" in their journey and search for the Christ Child and in defiance of King Herod.

Have you ever heard the expression "going out on a limb"? What do you suppose that means? If I were to climb a tree and then start crawling out toward the end of limb, what might happen? Right! The tree limb might break off and I would fall to the ground, perhaps injuring myself badly. Believe it or not, there is a true story about a man who was trimming a tree with a saw and he actually sawed off the limb he was sitting on! How silly is that?

So, to go out on a limb means taking a chance, taking a risk. And it has become an expression we use whenever we do something that is taking a chance or a risk. For instance, suppose a friend comes to me and asks me to sign a bank loan for him so he can buy a new car. If I do that and he decides to not pay the loan, then I am stuck with the loan and will have to pay for his new car. So to do that I would be taking a chance, taking a risk, going out on a limb.

Today's gospel reading is about a man who went out on a limb for Jesus. It is about Zacchaeus, the short little man who climbed the sycamore tree so he could see Jesus as he passed by. In doing that, Zacchaeus went out on a limb, literally. He took a chance of falling, didn't he? But he also took a chance of being embarrassed in front of the crowd. For it was not proper for a grown man to run and climb a tree like that.

Sometimes as followers of Jesus we are called to go out on a limb. That is, we are called to take a chance and risk embarrassment to do what we feel we need to do. Suppose a new student starts at your school and asks you to be her friend. Since you don't know the person, to become her friend would mean taking a chance, going out on a limb. But that is what Jesus would have us to do, isn't it? Sometimes we are called to take a little risk, to go out on a limb.

FOLLOW-UP: Brainstorm with the children other ways that they might safely go out on a limb as a follower of Jesus.

2
Your Little Light
One Small Light Can Make a Great Difference

SCRIPTURE: Luke 8:16 GNT

OBJECT FOR SHARING: A small, low-wattage light bulb

PRESENTATION: Plan this lesson for a Sunday during the season of Epiphany.

Good morning! I have brought a small light bulb with me today. At our house over our mantle we have some of these small lights; perhaps you have also seen them in chandeliers.

Well, recently one of those bulbs burned out. When I flipped on the switch, it went *Pow!* But the thing that surprised me was how dark it was after this one little bulb burned out. It was much more difficult to read the newspaper. So I was anxious to find a new bulb to put in its place.

This caused me to remember something that a preacher who lived long ago, named John Murray, said: "You may possess only a small light, but uncover it, let it shine, use it in order to bring more light and understanding to the hearts and minds of men and women" [and, of course, boys and girls].

Epiphany is the season of light. During this season we remember the wise men, or magi, who were guided by the light of a star to the place where the baby Jesus lay. But even more important is the light that God shared with all people when Jesus was revealed to the whole world.

But as we celebrate the season of light, it is important for every one of us to remember that we, too, have light to share with others. We have the light of kindness, the light of understanding to share with our family and friends, and we have the light of God's love to share.

So, as preacher John Murray says, you may think that you have only a small light, but uncover it, let it shine. As I learned recently, something very small like this can give off a lot of much needed light.

FOLLOW-UP: Illustrate with the children in a semidarkened room (being sensitive to those who may have a fear of or feel uneasy in the dark) the difference that one small light bulb or candle can make in the darkness. Invite them to brainstorm practical ways that they can let their lights shine.

3
Wade in the Water
Baptism Tells Us That God Makes Us Clean on the Inside

SCRIPTURE: Matthew 3:13–17 GNT

OBJECTS FOR SHARING: Photographs of the Jordan River, possibly with people being baptized, and of the Ganges River where people are bathing

PRESENTATION: Consider using the lesson on the Sunday when the baptism of Jesus is the scripture reading for the day, or on any Sunday when the sacrament of baptism is being administered.

Good morning! I have brought some pictures to share with you this morning. What do you think this is a picture of? (*Show each child a picture of the Jordan River*). This is a picture of the Jordan River, in Israel.

You know, since the beginning of time, people have been drawn to rivers. Why do you suppose that is? Correct. Many people get their drinking water from rivers. Some people go to the river to wash their clothes. Still others go to the river to take a bath and get all clean.

But many people also go to the river for religious or spiritual reasons. Here is another picture, of people going to the Ganges River in India to bathe as a part of their religious beliefs. *(Show each child a picture of Hindu worshipers bathing in the Ganges River.)* And here is a picture of people being baptized in the Jordan River.

You see, just as we might go to the river to wash our bodies outwardly to make them nice and clean, people have gone to the river to bathe and ask God to wash their hearts or souls and make them clean on the inside.

So in today's gospel reading we hear about Jesus going down to the Jordan River to be baptized, because that is what the people of his day were doing. By being baptized by John the Baptizer in the Jordan River, they believed God was washing away all the wrongs they had done. And today whenever we baptize anyone with water in our church, we are affirming God's promise to wash away all wrong from that person's life.

FOLLOW-UP: As the children return to their places, lead in singing "Wade in the Water."

4
A SUPER Bowl
Souper Bowl Sunday Is a Time to Help the Hungry of Our World

Scripture: Matthew 25:37–40 GNT

Object for Sharing: A very large bowl, as large as can be found, with a printed sign taped to the back with the word "SUPER Bowl," and a can of soup

Presentation: This lesson is intended for the Souper Bowl of Caring Sunday, usually the last Sunday of January or the first Sunday of February. You may want to have a familiar can of soup inside the bowl to hold up at the appropriate time.

You know what this is, don't you? Of course—this is a SUPER Bowl. See, it says it right here on the side—SUPER Bowl. One meaning of the word "super" is "superior in size." BIG. So this truly is a SUPER (BIG) bowl.

Of course we are thinking about a SUPER bowl because today is Super Bowl Sunday. This is the really big football game of the year, when two teams play for the national championship.

A few years ago (1990), a seminary student by the name of Brad Smith came up with the idea of making this a really big day in another way. The idea was to make this a really big SOUP day *(hold up can of soup)*, so they called it SOUPER Bowl Sunday. This could be a day to make soup and collect money in soup bowls for all the hungry of the world. The Souper Bowl of Caring began with this simple prayer: "God, even as we enjoy the Super Bowl football game, help us to be mindful of those who are without a bowl of soup to eat."

And today, I understand, you all are going to help sell and serve soup here at our church to raise money for local food pantries. So I want to encourage all of our adults in the congregation to plan on hanging around today to give their donation and eat the soup that has been prepared for us. Together, we can make this one SOUPER Bowl Sunday.

FOLLOW-UP: Plan in advance to have the children help in collecting donations, serve soup, pass out information about the Souper Bowl of Caring, and so on. By going to www.souperbowl.org one can request a Resource Kit, which includes posters, stickers, a DVD, and helpful instructions for planning a Souper Bowl of Caring event.

5
Time to Exercise!
Lent Is a Time for Spiritual Exercises

SCRIPTURE: Lamentations 3:40–41 GNT

OBJECTS FOR SHARING: Some arm weights, and maybe a jump rope or some exercise stretch bands

PRESENTATION: Ideally, this lesson would be presented on the first Sunday of Lent, but any Sunday in Lent would work.

Good morning! Everybody stand up. It's time for some exercise.

First, let's do a few jumping jacks to loosen up.

Okay, now let's bend over and touch our toes.

Finally, let's pretend we're lifting some arm weights.

Good. You can sit down and rest now.

Why are we talking about exercise this morning? Well, today is the first Sunday in Lent. The season of Lent is a time for *spiritual* exercises. What do physical exercises do for us? One thing is make us stronger, right? Well, spiritual exercises also make us stronger. They make us stronger disciples, or followers, of Jesus.

What are some spiritual exercises that we want to be more serious about during Lent? Prayer is one.

Reading the scriptures is another spiritual exercise. Or having a parent or grandparent read Bible stories to you.

Some people attend church more often during Lent. That is another spiritual exercise.

And then there is another spiritual exercise that you may have never heard about and that is not as popular. That is fasting. Can anyone tell us what fasting is? Fasting is going without food—missing a meal or two or three—in order to spend that time praying and asking God what one should do. Those who fast regularly say that the practice helps one's mind to be clearer and enables one to focus more on spiritual things and the things that really matter in life. For instance, many young persons get together once a year for a day-long fast and give the money they would have spent on food to hungry people in other parts of the world who don't have enough to eat.

Well, there is a gospel reading about a time Jesus went into the wilderness, where he fasted for forty days. I can't imagine that, can you? And while Jesus fasted, he prayed and asked God what he was supposed to do with his life.

And just like exercise makes one stronger in body, Jesus' fasting made him stronger on the inside.

So I would like to encourage you to do some spiritual exercises these next few weeks during the season of Lent. Exercise by spending some time praying, reading Bible stories or having someone read to you, by attending church every Sunday, and maybe even by keeping from eating something a time or two as you think about the hungry of the world. Through these spiritual exercises, you will become a stronger follower of Jesus.

FOLLOW-UP: Lead the children in doing some physical exercises (such as jumping jacks) while at the same time engaging in some spiritual exercises (such as praying short prayers).

6
Ways of Humble Service
Jesus Washing the Disciples' Feet Set an Example of Humble Service

SCRIPTURE: John 13:1–11 NRSV

OBJECTS FOR SHARING: Pitcher, basin, and towel

PRESENTATION: This lesson will work well near the end of Lent.

In the Bible, John tells of how Jesus, not long before his death, went around the table where he and his disciples were eating, and one by one he washed their feet and dried them with a towel. When he had finished, Jesus said, "If I, your Lord and Teacher, have washed your feet, you also ought to wash one another's feet. For I have set you an example, that you also should do as I have done to you" (John 13:12, 14).

Why do you think Jesus did that? Well, in that day and time, washing the feet of household guests or travelers was a common social practice. People walked where they were going. They traveled on dusty roads, either barefoot or wearing open sandals. If it was hot, their feet sweated; the dust caked on their feet and between their toes. It had to be uncomfortable.

So when someone traveled to your home, one of the first things you did was offer to wash his or her feet. It was an act of humble service and courtesy.

When someone comes to visit us today we say, "Let me take your coat," or "Could I get you something to drink?" It's the same principle, just a different approach.

So when Jesus said "you also should do as I have done to you," what he was really saying to those who would be his disciples was this: I have given you an example. As I have shown my love for you through this act of humble service, so you should show your love for one another and for the world through your acts of humble service.

And so, the lesson we take from this story is not that we have to literally wash other people's feet. Rather, Jesus calls us to be creative and think of ways that we can become humble and serve other people in Jesus' name. In what ways might we do that? We can help feed the hungry. We can welcome the poor or homeless to our worship and coffee hour. We can visit the sick and take them things that make them feel better. We can listen to people and let them know we love them when they are sad.

By serving other people, we do as Jesus did.

FOLLOW-UP: Plan a trip with the children so they can serve others through such means as cleaning up leaves from someone's lawn, baking cookies for elderly members or nursing home residents, and so on.

7
Learning to Be a Friend
One of the Best Things We Can Do Is Be a Friend to the Friendless

Scripture: John 15:14, 17 GNT

Object for Sharing: A picture of the devastation left by the Gulf Coast hurricanes in 2005 or of some other recent natural disaster (but hold until the end of the story)

Presentation: This story may be used on a special Friend Day or when a special offering is being emphasized, such as One Great Hour of Sharing.

"Children, this is Samantha. She has just moved here and will be in class with us from now on. You can take this seat here, Samantha," Ms. Wise said, pointing to an empty seat near the front of her fifth-grade classroom. "Now, let's take out our language books and get started."

Samantha was uncomfortable, since this was her first day in a new school. It didn't help matters that several of the other children kept staring at her throughout the morning. When lunchtime came, some of the children—boys and girls alike—gathered around her as they walked down the hall to the cafeteria. "You talk funny," one of the boys said to her. "Yeah, and you wear funny clothes; your jeans and your top don't match," one of the girls said to her. Samantha's face turned red, but she managed to hold in her tears and not cry.

Ms. Wise happened to hear the things that were said. "Samantha, since this is your first day, I think we will let you go to the head of the line. Eric, would you like to escort Samantha to the front of the line and show her the way?" she asked. Eric had been new at the school himself just a few weeks ago. Ms. Wise knew he could sympathize with Samantha and possibly make her a new friend. Then Ms. Wise went to the back of the line to the other children who had embarrassed Samantha about the way she talked and the clothes she was wearing. "Children, I have something to say to all of you, and I want you to listen well. A very wise person once said that we should always be kind to others, because we never know what kind of pain or suffering they might be having to bear.

"Would you like to know why Samantha talks differently than we do? And would you like to know why her outfit might not match perfectly? It is because Samantha just moved here from New Orleans. Her family's home was washed away by the hurricanes and floods. Samantha and her family are doing the best they can with a terrible situation. What Samantha really needs right now are some friends; some real good friends who let her know she is welcome here. Does anyone here think he or she can be a friend to Samantha?" Every child that heard what Ms. Wise had to say felt awful. How could they have been so thoughtless and rude? Slowly hands started to rise, indicating that they wanted to be a friend to Samantha who had moved so far away from the home she no longer had.

Not only did all the children of Ms. Wise's fifth grade class gain a new friend that day, but all of them also learned a valuable lesson—always be kind, because we never know the pain that others might be carrying.

FOLLOW-UP: Lead the children in collecting an offering or planning a fund-raiser for those affected by recent hurricanes, tornadoes, fires, or floods. They might also write letters to children to accompany the offering.

8
Solving the World's Problems
The Problems of the World Begin and End in the Heart

Scripture: Galatians 5:19–23 GNT

Objects for Sharing: A backpack that might be used for hiking or backpacking and a carved walking stick

Presentation: Consider sharing this lesson during the season of Lent, when the focus is on spiritual transformation.

There once was a man who became greatly troubled over the world's many problems. Every day when he read the newspaper and watched the evening news on television all he saw were problems, problems, problems. War, fighting, hatred based on race or religion, greed, some people having too much of the world's goods and others having nothing at all—all these things started to overwhelm this man. So he set out to find the one solution to the world's many problems.

The man had heard about a very wise religious philosopher who lived high up in the mountains. So he decided to go talk to the religious philosopher and see if he had an answer. So the man packed a backpack with enough food and water for several days, and then he set off. He climbed and climbed and climbed the mountain. It took him several days and nights to make it to the top. Finally he saw a small hut in the distance. *That must be where the wise religious philosopher lives*, he thought to himself.

The traveler approached the small hut and knocked on the door. A kind, gentle voice from inside said, "Enter." The traveler carefully opened the door. At a small table he saw a wise-looking man seated at a little table reading an open book and meditating. The wise man stood up and invited him to sit down. "I have come to ask you a very important question," the traveler said.

"Yes, we will discuss your question, but first you must eat." So the host went to his little stove and prepared the traveler something to eat and drink. After he had finished the food and drink, again the traveler said, "I have come to ask you a very important question."

"Yes, what is your question?" the wise man replied.

"I want to know," the traveler said, "wherein lies the solution to all the world's problems. War, fighting, hatred, greed, and the like. Surely there must be a solution to the problems that plague our world."

The wise man remained silent. Then he picked up a stick—a very beautifully carved walking stick that had all kinds of words engraved around it, words like love, joy, peace, kindness, compassion—and he put the end of the stick right up to the traveler's chest. Then the wise man said, "We will discuss your question, but first you must sleep." So the wise man took him over to the corner to a nice, clean mat on the floor. "Lie here and take a good rest," he said compassionately.

The next morning the sun coming up the mountain awakened the traveler. His host, the wise man, was already preparing breakfast. After they had eaten, again the traveler asked, "What about my very important question about the solution to the world's great problems?"

Again the wise man picked up the beautifully carved walking stick that had all the words like love, joy, peace, kindness, and compassion engraved on it. Again he touched the end of the stick to the man's chest. And then he said, "There is the solution to the world's great problems—within the human heart. Until every human heart is completely emptied of hatred and greed and then filled up again with love, joy, peace, kindness, and compassion, the problems of the world will never go away. So go back down the mountain and do whatever you can to get men and women, boys and girls to empty their hearts and then fill them back up again. And then you will solve the problems of the world."

So the traveler arose from the table, picked up his backpack, and trotted back down the mountain. And from that day forward he spent his life sharing with others the need to empty their hearts of hatred and greed and to fill them back up with love, joy, peace, kindness, and compassion. And now today, the man has spoken to us to do the same. Because we, too, can help solve the problems of the world.

FOLLOW-UP: Provide enough three-quarter-inch wooden dowels for the children to make their own "walking sticks" by using permanent markers to write the fruits of the Spirit (Gal. 5:22–23) around the edge.

9
Rolling Out the Red Carpet
We Show Respect to Jesus When We Welcome Others in His Name

SCRIPTURE: Matthew 21:6–9 GNT

OBJECT FOR SHARING: A piece of red carpet or red rug, even a red bathroom rug

PRESENTATION: This lesson is most appropriate for Palm Sunday.

Good morning! Do you see what I have brought with me today? Do you know what I am doing? I am rolling out the red carpet (*unroll the carpet or rug and lay it down in front of the children*). Does anyone know what "rolling out the red carpet" means? It means to extend a kingly welcome to someone.

Some people think that the practice of rolling out a red carpet actually began many centuries ago when a king was going to visit one of his subjects. So that the king would not have to walk on the ground and get his feet dirty, the man he was going to visit rolled a red carpet from his door to the king's carriage.

When might we see the red carpet rolled out today? That is correct—at some of the award shows on television they roll out the red carpet for movie stars. Also, when the President of the United States or the Queen of England pays a visit, the red carpet may be rolled out.

Do you think that the people rolled out the red carpet for Jesus on the day that he rode into Jerusalem on a donkey? In a manner of speaking they did when they cut palm branches from the trees and laid them and their coats on the road in front of him.

Well, Jesus is not here today for us to roll out the red carpet for him. But we can "roll out the red carpet" for others in his name, can't we? When new people come to our church for the first time we can try to give them a royal welcome by opening the door for them, by smiling at them and telling them how glad we are they came, by making sure that they get to be first at the line fellowship refreshments, and so on.

FOLLOW-UP: Lead the children in some role play, exploring different ways to "roll out the red carpet" for one another.

10
Easter Forgiveness
Jesus Shows Us How to Forgive Others

SCRIPTURE: Luke 23:32–38 GNT

OBJECT FOR SHARING: Any of the flowers commonly used at Easter that gives off a nice fragrance

PRESENTATION: Have a single flower in a small vase handy, but hold it until the right time in the story.

What do you think of when I say "Easter forgiveness"? (*Give time for answers.*) You have shared some good answers. Once when asked to define forgiveness, another child said, "Forgiveness is the scent flowers give when they are trampled on." I like that definition of forgiveness—"forgiveness is the scent flowers give when they are trampled on." Wow! That is powerful stuff, isn't it? If we were to step on any number of these flowers that grace our worship space this morning and crush them, they would smell all the stronger.

Well, I have been thinking that that is what Easter forgiveness is. Forgiveness as Jesus teaches us is not about hurting someone back who hurts us. It is not about getting even. It is not about holding a grudge and being mad at someone forever. The forgiveness that Jesus shows us in his life means responding in kindness, and love, and compassion. It means being sweet.

In the Bible we are told that when Jesus was crucified on the cross he prayed to God, "Forgive them, Father! They don't know what they are doing" (Luke 23:34). Like the flower that might be trampled upon, Jesus was being crushed. And yet, he was able to extend the sweetness of forgiveness to those who were crushing him.

And that, I think, is the Easter challenge that you and I are called to—to not repay evil for evil, hurt for hurt, but to learn how to forgive others who hurt us, because they may not know what they are doing.

"Forgiveness is the scent flowers give when they are trampled on."

FOLLOW-UP: Lead the children in smelling a variety of flowers common to the Easter season. If a botanist is available, perhaps she or he could discuss what gives flowers their fragrance.

11
Believing in What Is Not Seen
Many of the Important Things in Life Cannot Be Seen

SCRIPTURE: Hebrews 11:1 GNT

OBJECTS FOR SHARING: A pad of white paper and a white colored pencil

PRESENTATION: Conceal the artist's pencil in such a way and write the message in such a way that the color of the pencil cannot be seen. This lesson will work well on Easter Sunday or a day shortly thereafter.

Good morning! I have brought a pad of paper and a pencil and I am going to write a joyous message for you for this Easter season. (*Write "Happy Easter, everyone" in large letters on the pad of paper in such a way that the children cannot see what you have written until you turn it around and show it to them.*) There. Who would like to read what I have written? (*Expect a variety of responses, such as "You didn't write anything," or "You used invisible ink."*) Actually I did write a joyous Easter message for you. The message is there, I promise you. And this is what the message says: "Happy Easter, everyone." Just because you can't see it doesn't mean it isn't there. The reason you are having difficulty seeing the message is that I wrote it with a white pencil. If I had written the message on black construction paper, you could have read it immediately, couldn't you? But the truth is, the message is the same either way. Just because we can't see something doesn't mean it isn't true.

You know, that is really what the Easter season is about in many ways. Easter is about believing in things we can't see with our eyes. We didn't see Jesus rise from the dead. But as Christians we believe he did. We can't see Jesus sitting in our congregation today. But as Christians we believe his living presence is with us. We can't see life after death. But we believe it is so.

Someone wrote in the Bible, "To have faith is . . . to be certain of the things we cannot see." Some of the most important things in life that we believe in cannot be seen with our physical eyes. Rather, we see them with our hearts and we believe them to be true.

So, again (hold up pad of paper with the "Happy Easter, everyone" message written on it), happy Easter, everyone!

FOLLOW-UP: Brainstorm with the children some of the things we cannot see with our eyes but believe to be true.

12
Take a Hike
Walking and Talking with a Friend Is Good for Us

Scripture: Luke 24:13–35

Objects for Sharing: A small loaf of uncut bread and chalice of grape juice

Presentation: This lesson will work well one of the Sundays immediately after Easter.

___

Does anyone here enjoy taking a walk with a friend? (*Seek show of hands.*) Good. One of the things that I enjoy most is taking a walk with a friend, especially my *best* friend. Over the years, I have had some of my most important conversations while walking and talking with a friend. While walking with a friend you can talk about things that are troubling you, important decisions you have to make, or some Christian belief that you are struggling to understand, or you might share a dream you have for the future. There is just something about walking and talking together that causes it to be very good for us.

Luke, the writer of the third gospel, tells a story about how after Jesus' crucifixion and resurrection, two friends were walking and talking about something that was troubling them. These two friends were very sad, because their other friend, their teacher, had been crucified. Does anyone remember the story so that you can tell us what happened next? Luke says that the resurrected Jesus came along and started walking with them. But the two friends didn't recognize Jesus, since his appearance had been changed. And as the three of them walked together and talked about all that had happened and about the scriptures, they began to have a greater understanding.

So whenever you have the opportunity, I encourage all of you (adults included) to take a walk and a talk with a friend or family member. Walking and talking together is not only good for our physical health. It is good for our spiritual health as well.

FOLLOW-UP: Weather permitting, take the children on a nature hike. As you walk along, stimulate some conversation about God's creation and in what ways they might see evidence of God's activity in the world.

13
Moving That Stone
Sometimes Insurmountable Problems Can Be Solved

SCRIPTURE: John 11:1–44 GNT

OBJECT FOR SHARING: A basketball

PRESENTATION: Consider sharing this story during the season of Eastertide.

Do any of you like to play basketball? Shoot a few hoops? Here is a story about a father who wanted to erect a basketball goal for his children.

Several years ago, when his children were about your age, a man wanted to install a basketball goal for his children in the backyard where they were living. Since their lawn was quite hilly, there was only one level spot in the entire yard where he could even think about installing the basketball goal. But even this one level spot presented a problem. You see, right in the middle of that one spot was a big limestone rock. It was about the size of a large coffee table. And it stuck up out of the ground about eighteen inches high. There was no way he could install the basketball goal there, because the big rock was sticking up out of the ground right where the goal needed to go.

Well, one day the man was talking to his dad about the problem. And his dad said to him, "You can move that big rock if you want to." And the man replied, "What! Get out of here. You are pulling my leg." And his dad said, "No, I'm not kidding. You can move that rock if you really want to." Well, the man was willing to listen and see what his dad had to say. His dad said, "Gather a pile of dry wood and build a big fire on top of that rock. Get the rock real hot, and then take the water hose and spray it with cold water. Then build another fire on top of it and get it real hot again, and then spray it again with cold water. If you do that, the rock will crack, and you can take a big hammer and break it up and haul it off in a wheelbarrow."

Well, the man took his dad's advice and did as he suggested. And you know what? It worked. That big rock that stood in the way of installing a basketball goal was eventually moved. The man beat it up with a sledgehammer and hauled it away in a wheelbarrow. He then smoothed down the dirt where it had been and erected that basketball goal.

You see, sometimes obstacles that stand in our way and that can seem impossible actually can be moved, if we have a little bit of faith and put forth a little bit of effort. The gospel readings for the season of Easter tell stories of big rocks that seemed to be obstacles, that appeared to present impossible situations. There was a big rock that kept Lazarus hidden in the tomb where they had put him, and there was the big stone that was rolled over the tomb where Jesus was laid. But the good news of Easter is that, with God working in our lives, often the big stones that seem to make for impossible situations can be moved out of the way.

FOLLOW-UP: If possible, shoot some basketball with the children to help them remember the story.

14

Let's All Breathe Together
All Living Things on Earth Are Connected

SCRIPTURE: Genesis 1:11–12 GNT

OBJECT FOR SHARING: A green vine or other potted plant

PRESENTATION: This lesson will be excellent for Earth Day or Arbor Day.

Good morning. I bet that many of you have potted plants similar to this at your house. Have you ever thought about what we might have in common with potted plants like this?

One thing we have in common with this green plant is we both breathe. That's right. Plants and trees breathe in and out just like we do. However, there is a difference. What is the substance that we need to breathe in order to live? That's right—oxygen. And what do we breathe out? Cardon dioxide.

Now, what is it that plants breathe in? That's right—carbon dioxide. And what do plants breathe out? Oxygen.

What does this say to us? That humans and plants need each other. We provide plants with what they need to live, and plants provide us what we need to live. The bigger lesson that we learn from this is that all things in our world are interconnected and interdependent on one another.

Someone has said that 35 percent of the oxygen that we breath comes from the rainforests. But the sad thing is that every day the rainforests are being destroyed. They are being chopped down, to make paper and to clear land for farming. What does that say to us? That's right; one thing is to think of ways to use fewer paper products. What are some of the ways that we might cut back on our paper use?

When we plant and take care of green plants, we really are helping take care of ourselves, because we all are connected to everything else in creation. That means all living things need to work in harmony.

FOLLOW-UP: Lead the children in planting flowers, green plants, or, even better, a tree.

15
Peer Pressure
We Need to Remember Who We Are and to Be Strong

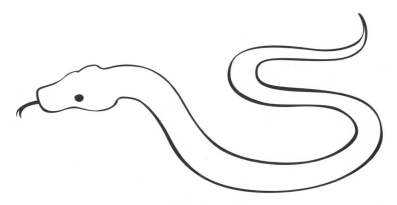

Scripture: Genesis 3:1–19 GNT

Object for Sharing: A stuffed or rubber (not too scary) snake to help you tell the story of Adam and Eve

Presentation: Warn the children before you bring out the rubber snake and let them know it is only a toy and they shouldn't be afraid.

How many of you have heard of "peer pressure"? Would anyone like to share what peer pressure means to you? Peer pressure is when a friend or someone else we know pressures us to do something that we really don't want to do. Often we know in our hearts that what someone is pressuring us to do is not right. And in many cases it might be harmful to us. It might even cause us to get sent to the principal's office, get suspended from school, or worse. Can you think of some things that someone might try to pressure you to do that you know would not be right?

The first chapters of the Bible tell the story of Adam and Eve and how peer pressure got them into big trouble. The story tells how that way back at the beginning of creation, the man and woman got along wonderfully with all the animals of the world, even the serpent or snake. At that time they were not afraid of the snake like many of us are today. So one day, the snake came along (remove rubber snake from your mystery bag) and started pressuring the woman and the man to do something God had told them not to do. "But we're not supposed to do *that!*" the woman replied to the snake.

But the snake was clever and quite persuasive. "Oh, come on," the snake said. "You won't get into trouble; I promise." So the snake kept on putting pressure on the man and woman until finally they gave in and did what they knew in their hearts they really should not do. Well, what happened? Adam and Eve were forced to leave the beautiful Garden of Eden, and forever after that their lives were filled with all kinds of trouble.

That's the way it is when we let others pressure us into doing something we know in our hearts we shouldn't do. When others pressure us to do things we know we shouldn't do, we always need to think about the consequences of our actions. We should ask, "Could this harm me? Could this get me into trouble?" And one of the best things that we can do is remember the good person we really are inside and not let ourselves be dragged down to becoming a lesser person than we know we should be.

FOLLOW-UP: Brainstorm with the children about things that others might pressure them to do that would not be good.

16
A Drink of Water, Please
Worship Is Like a Refreshing Drink of Spiritual Water

SCRIPTURE: Psalm 42:1–2 GNT

OBJECTS FOR SHARING: A small green plant, perhaps a vine, and a small watering can or pitcher

PRESENTATION: Try to find a green plant that appears to be neglected and in need of water.

I have brought with me today one of my green plants. Now, I have a confession to make. Sometimes I am not very kind to my green plants. Often I let them go too long without giving them a drink. And when I do, they start to wilt and look lifeless, and they may even start to turn yellow. We all know that plants need life-giving water to stay alive and healthy.

Sometimes during the week when I see a peace lily I notice that it may be wilted and all flopped over toward the floor. When a peace lily looks like that, what is wrong with it? That is correct—it needs a good drink of water. The thing about peace lilies is they can be all wilted and flopped over toward the floor, but when you give them a good drink of water, in no time at all they will be standing up tall and proud again. It is amazing, isn't it?

You know, we are sort of like that too. Especially in the summertime when it is really hot outside and we perspire a lot we can start feeling all droopy and wilted like a green plant. But a cool drink of water can perk us right up again.

But there is another way of looking at this as well. Sometimes our spirits start to feel droopy or wilted too. We start feeling really down inside, discouraged, sad, lonely, or maybe even hopeless. But then we can come here to worship where we pray, sing joyful songs to God, hear an encouraging word from our Sunday school teacher or the pastor, and we start to feel strong and alive again. It is like we have had a drink of spiritual water, living water, that has picked us up again. That is one of the benefits of coming together every week for worship. We receive a good drink of living water that enables us to stand tall and proud the rest of the week. (*Water the green plant as the children exit.*)

FOLLOW-UP: Let the children share in watering any available green plants. Then talk with them about the aspects of worship that make them feel alive again.

17
I Was Blind,
But Now I See
Learning Is a Lifelong Process

SCRIPTURE: John 9:1–25 GNT

OBJECT FOR SHARING: A pair of dark glasses like those often worn by the blind

PRESENTATION: Consider showing at the close of the presentation a video clip from the 2006 movie *Amazing Grace* about William Wilberforce and John Newton and their crusade to end slave trafficking in England.

A long, long time ago, there lived in England a young man whose name was John. John's father was a sea captain, so it was only natural that he would follow in his father's footsteps and go to sea. So at the age of eleven, John began sailing with his father. After his father retired, John continued to sail. Once, while John was aboard a ship named "Greyhound," the ship got caught in a severe storm and was in danger of sinking. John awoke in the middle of the night and found that the ship was filling up with water. So he prayed to God to be saved. This was the time that he remembered as the beginning of his Christian life. And so John began to read the Bible and any other religious literature he could find. He determined to live a good, clean life.

But there was one big mistake in John's life that took him a long time to give up. John, you see, was a slave trader. He helped sail ships that went to Africa and kidnapped people from their homes and villages and then took them to other countries where they were sold as slaves. John would later say that his true religious change did not happen until some time later. One of the things that John's life teaches us is that becoming the person God wants us to be doesn't just happen overnight. It is an ongoing process, something that we need to work on every day. Well, eventually John came to see that selling people as slaves was wrong. During a serious illness John determined that he would no longer be involved in the transport or selling of slaves. Instead, he started to study so that he could become a minister and preach. It is said that John was such a good preacher that great crowds flocked to the churches to hear him. In one place they had to add on to the church so it would be big enough to hold the crowd that wanted to hear him preach.

After becoming a minister, John began working with his good friend, William, to put an end to slave trading in England. And that is what they did. But the thing that John is most remembered for is the hymn that he wrote that is known and loved by people all over the world. That hymn is "Amazing Grace." It is based on the story in the Bible of Jesus healing the man born blind. In that hymn, John Newton tells the story of how God opened his eyes so that he was able to see what God wanted him to do. "I once was lost, but now am found, was blind but now I see."

One of the reasons that people love the hymn "Amazing Grace," I believe, is because almost everyone has felt or longed for God's grace at work in their lives. And that is the story of John Newton and the hymn "Amazing Grace."

FOLLOW-UP: Lead in singing "Amazing Grace" as the children return to their places.

18
Soul Food
Just as Our Bodies Need Food, So Do Our Spirits

SCRIPTURE: Psalm 23 NRSV

OBJECTS FOR SHARING: Bible, books on spirituality (such as *Care of the Soul, Let Your Life Speak*), a hymnal, a book of poetry, a nature picture

PRESENTATION: Consider bringing a small side table into the worship space and arranging the items suggested in a "soulful" manner.

Good morning! Can anyone tell us what "soul food" is? Well, the way we answer might depend on what part of the country we come from. In some places, southern states to give an example, the term "soul food" is used to mean certain types of food one might eat, such as collard greens, sweet potato pie, barbecued ribs, and so on.

But we could also look at the term "soul food" in another way. We could think about it being food for our souls or spirits, that invisible part of us inside that thinks, feels, loves, learns, and so on. Just as our physical bodies need food, so do our souls. Has your soul ever been hungry? How might we know that our soul is hungry? Can you think of some things we might use to feed our souls?

Well, I have brought some soul food with me this morning to give you some examples. For many years the Bible has been a source of soul food to me. And then I have a book titled *Care of the Soul* and another one titled *Let Your Life Speak*. And here is a book of poetry that has some really good soul food. And what about a hymn book? For many of us singing hymns is a form of soul food.

Another source of soul food for me is nature, the great outdoors. Since I couldn't bring the great outdoors inside this morning, I brought a picture to show you.

One more very important type of soul food is worship. As we gather here to sing, pray, fellowship, and learn together, our souls are fed for another week.

All of these things and more can serve as soul food for us and can feed our souls when they are hungry. And there is nothing worse than a hungry, growling soul. Right?

FOLLOW-UP: Invite the children to share places they have visited (mountains, shore, etc.) that helped feed their souls.

19
Filled with the Spirit
We Can Make Room for the Spirit's Presence

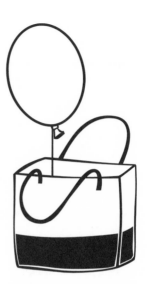

SCRIPTURE: Galatians 5:22–23 NRSV

OBJECTS FOR SHARING: A "mystery bag" containing a number of quite small, light-colored balloons with a different vice such as "anger, fighting, hatred, stealing, lying," and so on written on each; a larger, red balloon with "Spirit" written on it with a black magic marker in large letters and "love, joy, peace, patience, kindness, generosity, faithfulness, gentleness, and self-control" written around it in small letters; finally, a tall, clear water pitcher suitable for putting the balloons in so the children can see them. The "Spirit" balloon should be just big enough to fill the pitcher.

PRESENTATION: This story will work well on or just after Pentecost Sunday.

I invite you to use your imagination today. Consider that this pitcher is your life. Can you imagine that with me? Okay. As we go through life we are tempted to allow our lives to fill up with all kinds of things. Many of these things are not very attractive. For instance, one of the things that we can allow into our lives is anger (*remove small balloon with "anger" written on it from the mystery bag and place it in the pitcher*).

Another thing we can allow into our lives is fighting (*remove small balloon with "fighting" written on it from the mystery bag and place it in the pitcher*).

Hatred is another thing we can let slip into our lives (*remove small balloon with "hatred" written on it from the mystery bag and place it in the pitcher*).

And then there is stealing (*remove small balloon with "stealing" written on it from the mystery bag and place it in the pitcher*).

And what about lying? Isn't that something else we can allow into our lives? (*Remove small balloon with "lying" written on it from the mystery bag and place it in the pitcher. Continue with other like habits until the pitcher is full*).

So you see, pretty soon, if we are not careful, our lives are full of all kinds of unattractive habits. But we have left out something very important. That very important something is the Spirit. The Holy Spirit. The God Spirit. Look what happens if we try to allow the Spirit into our life when it is full of all those other unattractive habits. The Spirit can't get in. In fact, the Spirit won't come in when we allow our lives to be filled with things like anger, fighting, hatred, stealing, lying, and such.

How much better to empty our lives of the unattractive habits (*pour or remove all the balloons from the pitcher*) and let the Spirit fill our lives (*place the red "Spirit" balloon in the pitcher*). When the Spirit fills our lives, we are also filled with the gifts of love, joy, peace, patience, kindness, generosity, faithfulness, gentleness, and self-control.

Being filled with the Spirit—that's what the season of Pentecost is all about. And being filled with the Spirit is what makes our lives so beautiful.

FOLLOW-UP: Lead the children in creating pictures (with crayons, watercolors, hand paints, etc.) that depict the Spirit's positive activity in life or the world.

20
The Proof Is in the Fruit
We Are Each Called to Bear Quality Spiritual Fruit

SCRIPTURES: Matthew 12:33 GNT; Luke 13:6–9 GNT

OBJECTS FOR SHARING: Two apples—a big, bright, red, delicious-looking one, and a small, hard, knotty one.

PRESENTATION: This story will work well during Pentecost season.

"Dad, what are you doing?" Monica asked her father as she approached him in his apple orchard. Her dad was down on his knees sawing at the base of an apple tree.

"Well, Monica, I'm cutting down this apple tree."

"But why, Dad? Why would you want to cut down a perfectly good tree?"

"That's a very good question, Monica. Let me see if I can explain." Monica's dad laid his saw down on the ground as he stood up. He walked over to another apple tree and pulled off a big, shining red apple. Then he walked back to the tree where the saw lay and pulled off a small, rough, knotty piece of fruit. Monica's dad held one apple in each hand and extended them toward Monica. "Okay—which apple would you choose? The big, shining red apple, or the small, hard, knotty one?"

"Oh, Daddy, the big pretty one, of course."

"You're exactly right, Monica. You see, that tree over there is a healthy tree; it bears good fruit. But this tree here, well, something happened along the way and it became unhealthy. It bears bad fruit. So it is no good. It is just taking up space in my orchard. So I am cutting it down so that I can plant another tree that will bear good fruit. Now do you understand?"

"Yes, I think I understand." Monica retreated into deep thought as though she was pondering another question.

"Is something else on your mind, Monica?" her dad asked.

"Well, I remember something the pastor said a few Sundays ago about each of us bearing fruit. Now I think I understand what he was talking about. In order for us to bear good fruit, we have to be like a good tree, don't we?"

"Monica, you are wise beyond your years. You are exactly right. To bear good spiritual fruit on the outside requires that we be spiritually healthy on the inside. That is why we spend time in prayer, studying the scriptures, and going to church—so that we can learn how to be more loving, forgiving, compassionate, and kind. For these are the things that make us spiritually healthy and able to bear good spiritual fruit."

FOLLOW-UP: Secure and make plans to plant a fruit tree with the children's help, being careful to follow the seller's instructions for proper planting. As you plant the tree, explain to the children that it takes time for a young fruit tree to mature to bear fruit, just as Christian maturation is a process that takes time and doesn't happen overnight. This illustrates the need for ongoing spiritual learning and spiritual formation.

21

Your Favorite Shirt Color
Just as We Change What We Look Like on the Outside, We Should Also Change the Inside

SCRIPTURE: Romans 12:2 GNT

OBJECTS FOR SHARING: A variety of different-colored blouses or shirts.

PRESENTATION: This story will work well during Pentecost when being transformed by the Spirit is being celebrated. Consider planning this activity just before a group trip so the children can wear the shirts they have created, if they choose.

What is your favorite shirt or blouse color? I don't know that I really have a favorite shirt color. Sometimes, on days when I am on official church business or want to feel dressed up, I may wear a white shirt. Other days, like when I am going for a walk in the neighborhood, I may wear a plain blue shirt. If I plan to take a hike in the woods, I may put on a tan shirt. But if I am going to church camp, I may decide to wear my shirt that has our church's name written on it. Sometimes I may put on one shirt and then change my mind and put on another one.

We are all the time changing what we look like on the outside, aren't we? And whether I decide to wear a blue shirt or then change my mind and put on a green shirt is not that important, is it?

But what is important is the change that is taking place on the inside. Just as we change what we look like on the outside, we should be changing on the inside as well. And changing what we look like on the inside is not as easy as changing what we look like on the outside. Actually, changing what we look like on the inside is a life-long task. We should be changing on the inside every day as long as we live. Every day we should be changing so that we are becoming more loving, more forgiving, more compassionate, and more helpful to others. That is what being a follower of Jesus and a member of the church is all about. It is learning how to be more like Jesus and the followers he calls us to be.

So, whenever you change your shirt or your blouse, let it be a reminder of the change that is taking place on the inside as well.

FOLLOW-UP: What a great opportunity to let children decorate their own shirt with tie dying or permanent markers. Have one tee shirt for each child and a suitable space for decorating.

22
God's Stamp of Approval
In Baptism, We Are Marked as God's Children

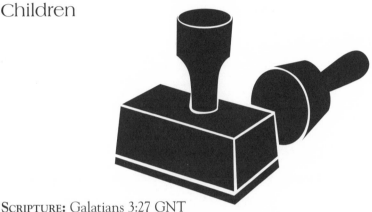

SCRIPTURE: Galatians 3:27 GNT

OBJECTS FOR SHARING: Rubber name stamp and inkpad

PRESENTATION: This story will work well on a day when a child or adult is being baptized.

I am sure that you have seen one of these. Whenever I buy a new book, I usually take my rubber stamp and stamp the inside front page. Sometimes I also stamp the bottom edge of the book, like this *(stamp the bottom edge for the children to see)*. Why do you think I do this? Correct. By stamping the book it lets everyone know that the book belongs to me. This is my mark. So if I forget and leave the book somewhere, or if I loan the book to someone, my name is in plain view for everyone to see so it can find its way home again.

Well, today we are going to put a stamp upon one of our members. Could anyone guess what that stamp might be? It is the stamp or mark of baptism. Baptism is God's stamp upon a person—a baby or a child or an adult—that says this person belongs to me. This is my child. When we pour water on the head and make the sign of the cross on someone's forehead, we are acting on God's behalf and putting God's stamp upon that person. Everyone here will see and celebrate. And from this day on, that person will look back and remember his or her baptism and be reminded of God's mark placed upon him or her as a child of God.

FOLLOW-UP: Secure rubber stamps (perhaps of butterflies, which symbolize new life) and perhaps small inkpads for the children to enjoy.

23

My Name Is David

God Can Use Anyone, No Matter How Young, to Accomplish God's Purpose

SCRIPTURE: 1 Samuel 16:1, 5, 10–13 GNT

OBJECT FOR SHARING: A picture or statue of a shepherd boy

PRESENTATION: This story will work well on Children's Sunday (for most churches a Sunday in June), or in conjunction with the lectionary reading of David being anointed king, or on a Sunday when Psalm 23 is read. For dramatic purposes, the presenter may want to don a shepherd's clothing and carry a shepherd's staff.

My name is David. The eighth son of Jesse of Bethlehem. A shepherd boy, a keeper of sheep on the hillsides of Judea. Sometimes while lying in the green grass watching the sheep, I write poems and songs of praise to the God of Israel to pass the time.

I am a young man, not much more than a child.

I am dark of complexion from spending so much time in the sun taking care of my father's sheep. Some say I am a skilled player of the harp, and that the music I play has a calming effect upon all who hear it. Others say that I am handsome and have beautiful eyes. But what can I know? I am little more than a child.

So you can imagine how shocked I was when I was called in from the fields and chosen to be a leader in Israel. There I was in the far pasture, the one by the stream, daydreaming as the sheep grazed and I composed psalms in my heart. Then without warning this messenger arrived; he startled me. I'd been summoned to appear at my father's house. *What can this mean?* I kept asking myself as I ran through the fields. *There must be some kind of trouble back at home. Perhaps father has taken ill, or one of my brothers has been involved in an accident.* But no, I learned it was nothing like that.

When I arrived, everyone was waiting on me. Waiting on ME, the youngest and the smallest of them all. My father and seven brothers were there, and this prophet named Samuel whom I did not know. And before I knew it, Samuel was pouring olive oil on my head, anointing me king of Israel, he said. Can you imagine that? Me, little more than a child, being anointed God's king of Israel! Who was I to be anointed king? My brother, Eliab, he was the most logical one to become king, if anyone from our family was to be. Good looking and tall, and being the oldest, he was the apparent heir, the one to whom any such honor should rightly fall. How absurd that I, the youngest and smallest, should be chosen for such an extraordinary honor!

And why was our family chosen for such an honor anyway? We have no pedigree to be proud of. There are plenty of skeletons in our family closest; ugly knots are abundant on our family tree. My great-grandmother was Ruth, an immigrant Moabite woman. My great-grandfather was Boaz, whose ancestors included Tamar, a Canaanite woman who was almost executed for being unfaithful to her husband, and Rahab, another Canaanite woman with a bad reputation from Jericho. Who am I, a small, lowly shepherd boy from an imperfect family to become king of Israel? Perhaps the God of Israel sees something that I cannot see.

God, I am told, has a different way of seeing things than we do. God, it is said, cares not where we have come from or where we have been. And God often chooses to use what is small and insignificant to accomplish divine purposes in the world.

We mortals settle for outward appearance. And we can be so fooled by appearances. But appearance alone is woefully inadequate. We often fail to see the possibilities of grace and hope because we are not seeing in the right way. God, on the other hand, can find possibilities for grace in life's most unexpected places and in some of the most unexpected persons. Why, I bet God could even find great possibilities in a child born among sheep in a stable. Sometimes with God the first shall be last, and the last shall be first.

Because, you see, God looks at the inside, at the heart. God sees deeper into our inward condition, much deeper than can be seen by the world. God is concerned with the will and character of a person. In the end, that is what matters most. And God sees possibilities in us, even when others do not. There's the most important thing—"seeing." Samuel, the prophet, at first was not properly seeing, I am told. He at first wanted to anoint my brother Eliab. But God had to show Samuel that he was seeing wrongly. He was looking at outward appearances and not seeing into the heart. Blushingly I admit that it has been said of me that I am a man after God's own heart. Perhaps that is why God chose me to be the new king of Israel—because God saw what was in my heart.

The good news is that God's grace extends to all—to the outsider, the underdog, the outcast, and the little person. No matter how humble, no matter how young, and no matter how small we might be, God's grace and God's possibilities take shape in those who allow God to use them. When we give our hearts to God—when we are willing to be men and women, boys and girls after God's own heart, then God can use us in extraordinary ways. Why, with a devoted heart, even a lowly, small shepherd boy like me can be used of God in a mighty way.

My name is David. The eighth son of Jesse of Bethlehem. A shepherd boy, a keeper of sheep on the hillsides of Judea. I am a young man, not much more than a child. But with God, all things are possible. With God, even a little child can lead the world.

FOLLOW-UP: Discuss with children how each of us can use Bible stories and our imaginations to read between the lines and explore important biblical ideas through biblical characters.

24
Little But Large
Little Things Are Just as Important as Big Things

SCRIPTURE: Luke 18:15–17 GNT

OBJECT FOR SHARING: A digital camera card

PRESENTATION: This story might be considered on Children's Day or when an infant baptism is planned.

I have brought with me this morning something very small (*hold up the digital card for all to see*). Does anyone have any idea what this tiny object is? This is a digital memory card that goes in my camera. You may not believe it, but I can have 180 color pictures on this tiny card. Can you imagine that? It just blows my mind to think about it! Now don't ask me to explain it, but it is true. Some small electronic cards this size can hold hundreds of pictures or thousands of pages of information. This just goes to show that something doesn't have to be big to be important.

You know, it's that way with people, too. A person doesn't have to be a big person to be important. The smallest people in the world, according to Jesus, are the most important! Those who are like children are the largest, the greatest in God's world. And you know who that includes? It includes *you!* You are very important to Jesus, and you are very important to this church. There is something special about each one of you. And each one of you has something good to share with the world.

Now, just so you will know that I am telling you the truth, I want to add your picture to my tiny little picture card. So can everyone sort of squeeze together and smile real big for me? (*Take the picture, and then show the image to each of the children*).

How important that little picture card is. But how much more important are you.

FOLLOW-UP: Print copies of the group picture so each child can take one home.

25

Are We Ever Alone?
God (Divine Presence) Is Everywhere

Scripture: Psalm 139:7–12 GNT

Object for Sharing: A globe on which can be pointed out Antarctica and the South Pole

Presentation: Although this story could work well anytime, it might be considered for "nature Sunday" or near the end of the church school year when some children are thinking about vacations and/or summer camp.

What do you think is the coldest, most desolate place in the world? (*Give opportunity for replies.*) Those are all good answers. Most people think of the North Pole as being the coldest, most desolate place on earth. But you know, it is just as cold and desolate, maybe even more so, at the South Pole (*point out the South Pole on the globe*). Imagine, if you can, spending the winter at the South Pole, the coldest and most forsaken place on earth, and spending it alone! All by yourself! With no one else to talk to or keep you company!

Yet, that is exactly what a man by the name of Admiral Richard Byrd did. In 1934, Admiral Byrd took a group of 56 men to Antarctica (the South Pole) to spend the winter. Admiral Byrd himself went 123 miles farther than the rest of the group. And for five months, Byrd lived by himself in a tiny hut in that unknown part of the world.

While at the South Pole, Admiral Byrd sat down in his hut and wrote these words: "Though I am cut off from human beings, I am not alone."

What do you suppose Admiral Byrd meant? "Though I am cut off from human beings, I am not alone." I think Admiral Byrd might have meant that though he was completely separated from everybody else in the world, he could feel the Divine Presence, the presence of God.

One of the messages of the Bible is that God is everywhere. And God never leaves us alone. No matter where we might go in this world, or in this universe, the presence of God is always with us.

We probably will never go as far away as Admiral Byrd did, to a completely frozen part of the world where no other people are. But sometimes it is good for all of us to go away by ourselves to a park, nature preserve, or church camp where we can be alone and experience, like Admiral Byrd did, the presence of God.

FOLLOW-UP: Lead the children in reading and discussing Psalm 139 from one of the contemporary translations of the Bible, and encourage them to use their imaginations to suggest places where God might be found.

26
No Vacation for God
We Can Remember God, Even When Away from Church

SCRIPTURE: Lamentations 3:22–23 NRSV

OBJECTS FOR SHARING: Toys appropriate to vacation time, such as beach balls, beach mat, snorkel, camping gear, and the like.

PRESENTATION: This story will work best on the last Sunday of the school year, just before the beginning of the summer schedule.

Do you know what time it is? It is vacation time! It is time for school to be out. It is time to go swimming and take family trips to the mountains, beach, or lakeshore. It is time to go on vacation.

But even though we may be away from church for a while and go on vacation, God doesn't take a vacation from us. While we are away having fun, God continues to provide for us. The sun continues to shine, making things grow. Streams continue to flow, providing us with water to drink. Fruits and vegetables continue to grow, providing us with food. God's work is never done.

Have you ever stopped to think about what would happen if God decided to quit working and take a vacation? It would be disastrous. I don't even want to think about it. But we don't have to worry about that happening, because in all the years since creation began, God has never taken a vacation.

So, even though we may be away from our church for a while, it doesn't mean that we have to take a vacation from God. During the summer, while we are away, we can still read the Bible or have our parents or grandparents read Bible stories to us. We can still pray every day. We can visit other churches in other towns on Sunday. And we can still send an offering to church. I am sure that our treasurer would be more than happy to receive it.

So I hope that you and your family have a wonderful time together this summer. I hope you get to take some fun vacations.

But I also hope that during these summer months we will still remember to worship God. Because God never takes a vacation from us.

FOLLOW-UP: Encourage the children to share what they would like to do with their families during the summer. These thoughts might be shared with their families later. Consider having the children discuss the words of a hymn that speak of God's providential care, such as "I Sing the Mighty Power of God," "This Is My Father's World," or "Great Is Thy Faithfulness."

Annotated Resources

Anderson, Herbert, and Foley, Edward. *Mighty Stories, Dangerous Rituals: Weaving Together the Human and the Divine*. San Francisco: Jossey-Bass, 1998.
　　Discusses the power of religious ritual and myth and how they help us create and express meaning. Shows how ritual and myth connect the human and divine.

Bettelheim, Bruno. *The Uses of Enchantment: The Meaning and Importance of Fairy Tales*. New York: Alfred A. Knopf, 1976.
　　An invaluable resource in the theory of how children's tales should arouse curiosity, stimulate the imagination, help children discover their self-identity and deal with inner conflicts, and confront their fears and problems.

Cameron, Julia. *The Artist's Way*. New York: G.P. Putnam's Sons, 1992.
　　Cameron seeks, through practical guidance, to bring out the creative energy, what she refers to as "God energy," that is within all of us.

Campbell, Joseph, with Bill Moyers. *The Power of Myth*. New York: Doubleday, 1988.
　　This work highlights exactly what the title suggests: the power of religious myths. Much is said about the hero that "lurks in each one of us."

Coles, Robert. *The Spiritual Life of Children*. Boston: Houghton Mifflin Company, 1990.
　　A wealth of wisdom has been gleaned and shared from Coles' interviews with hundreds of children from a number of religious backgrounds. This work reveals the great depth of thought in religious matters that children are capable of when given a chance to express themselves.

Estes, Clarissa Pinkola, ed. *Tales of the Brothers Grimm*. New York: Quality Paperback Book Club, 1999.
　　In her introduction to the *Tales of the Brothers Grimm*, Estes discusses soul life, innate ideals, and universal thoughts. A good resource for those interested in universal thoughts and archetypes.

Fahs, Sophia L. *Jesus the Carpenter's Son*. Boston: Beacon Press, 1945.
　　Fahs uses the imagination (and indirectly encourages the modern presenter of children's sermons) to fill in the blanks and address the "What ifs" that surround the life of Jesus.

Fahs, Sophia. L. *Today's Children and Yesterday's Heritage.* Boston: Beacon, 1952.
In this work Fahs stresses the importance of a child's self-worth, the child's sense of relationship with the larger world, the need to "feel the Mystery of Life," and the interdependence of all life.

Groome, Thomas H. *Christian Religious Education.* San Francisco: Harper Collins, 1980.
Groome speaks of the importance of lived faith, becoming what we are called to become, and nurturing human freedom and creativity.

Hammer, Randy. *Everyone a Butterfly: 40 Sermons for Children.* Boston: Skinner House Books, 2004.
In addition to forty children's sermons that follow the church year beginning in September and ending in June, this collection includes an introduction that discusses the theory of sermon preparation for children and what makes for a "successful" children's sermon. Each entry includes a suggested object for sharing, suggestions for presentation, and possible follow-up activities.

Hammer, Randy. *The Singing Bowl: 26 Children's Sermons with Activities.* Cleveland: Pilgrim Press, 2007.
Following the same format as the present volume, the stories and lessons in *The Singing Bowl* include stories and lessons that may be used for special Sundays such as Reign of Christ Sunday, the Sunday near Thanksgiving, Sundays during Advent and Epiphany, the Sunday near Martin Luther King Jr.'s birthday, and on days when Holy Communion or baptism will be celebrated or when there will be or an emphasis on stewardship or missions.

Hammer, Randy. *The Talking Stick: 40 Children's Sermons with Activities.* Cleveland: Pilgrim Press, 2007.
Following the same format as the present volume, the forty stories and lessons in *The Talking Stick* generally follow the church calendar. A number of them aquaint listeners with historic figures, such as Brother Lawrence, Martin Luther, and Phyllis Wheatley. The stories encourage respect for everyone created in the divine image and seek to instill such positive qualities as service, hospitality, unity, stewardship of the earth, truthfulness, peacemaking, and the like.

Handford, S. A., translator. *Aesop's Fables.* New York: Penguin, 1994.
Brief moral tales, many of which can easily be adapted for use with children in worship. In the introduction, Handford discusses the "common-sense and folk wisdom" at the heart of stories and fables.

Harris, Maria. *Fashion Me a People.* Louisville: Westminster John Knox Press, 1989.
Harris notes the importance of spending time alone "in the company of the Divine."

Jordan, Jerry Marshall. *Filling Up the Brown Bag* (a children's sermon how-to book).

New York: Pilgrim Press, 1987.

An invaluable resource, Jordan stresses the importance of letting children know they are loved and wanted, nurturing within them an awareness of God, instilling within them a sense of self-worth and a positive self-image, encouraging them to stretch themselves and reach their full potential, and sparking their imaginations by getting them to say "I see!"

MacDonald, Margaret Read. *The Story-Teller's Start-Up Book: Finding, Learning, Performing and Using Folktales*. Little Rock, Ark.: August House, 1993.

A very helpful work that gives practical guidance on finding, preparing, and telling folktales and other stories.

Rogers, Fred. *Play Time*. Philadelphia: Running Press, 2001.

A good resource, most notably for preschoolers, for planning follow-up activities utilizing common household objects. Encourages children's use of imagination and creativity.

Rogers, Fred. *You Are Special*. Philadelphia: Running Press, 2002.

A tiny pocket book of timeless wisdom that reinforces the truth that everyone is special and that can easily be worked into many children's sermons.

Sawyer, Ruth. *The Way of the Storyteller*. New York: Penguin, 1970.

This work is a well-known classic on the art of storytelling that should be read by everyone who has a real interest in storytelling.

Silf, Margaret, ed. *Wisdom Stories from Around the World*. Cleveland: Pilgrim Press, 2003.

Though written primarily from an adult viewpoint, many of these wonderful stories can be adapted for use with children.

Wagner, Betty Jane. *Dorothy Heathcote: Drama as a Learning Medium*. Rev. ed. Portland, Me.: Calendar Islands Publishers, 1999.

Though written as a resource for leading children in drama, this is also a good resource—especially the first half—on how to physically lead children's sermons. Discusses the discovery of human experience, reaching a deeper insight, helping children catch a vision of the wider world, and the importance of tapping the energy of the human spirit and valuing human achievement.

Supply List

Chapter 1: Going Out on a Limb
🖐 Limb (as big as practical) from a tree

Chapter 2: Your Little Light
🖐 Small, low-wattage light bulb

Chapter 3: Wade in the Water
🖐 Photos of Jordan and Ganges Rivers

Chapter 4: A SUPER Bowl
🖐 Large mixing bowl
🖐 Can of soup
🖐 Souper Bowl of Caring materials

Chapter 5: Time to Exercise!
🖐 Arm weights
🖐 Jump rope
🖐 Exercise bands

Chapter 6: Ways of Humble Service
🖐 Pitcher
🖐 Basin
🖐 Towel

Chapter 7: Learning to Be a Friend
🖐 Photos of devastation by natural disasters

Chapter 8: Solving the World's Problems
🖐 Backpack

- 🖐 Carved walking stick
- 🖐 Three-quarter-inch wooden dowels
- 🖐 Permanent markers

Chapter 9: Rolling Out the Red Carpet
- 🖐 Red rug or piece of red carpet

Chapter 10: Easter Forgiveness
- 🖐 Fragrant flower in a vase

Chapter 11: Believing in What Is Not Seen
- 🖐 Pad of white paper
- 🖐 White colored pencil

Chapter 12: Take a Hike
- 🖐 Small loaf of uncut bread
- 🖐 Chalice of grape juice

Chapter 13: Moving That Stone
- 🖐 Basketball

Chapter 14: Let's All Breathe Together
- 🖐 Green vine or potted plant
- 🖐 Flowers, plant, or tree for children to plant

Chapter 15: Peer Pressure
- 🖐 Stuffed or toy rubber snake

Chapter 16: A Drink of Water, Please
- 🖐 Green (wilted) plant
- 🖐 Watering can or pitcher

Chapter 17: I Was Blind, But Now I See
- 🖐 Dark glasses
- 🖐 Video clip from the movie *Amazing Grace*

Chapter 18: Soul Food
- Bible
- Books on spirituality
- Book of poetry
- Hymnal
- Nature picture

Chapter 19: Filled with the Spirit
- "Mystery bag"
- Large, clear water pitcher
- Variety of small light-colored balloons
- Larger, red balloon (should fit into and fill pitcher)
- Permanent markers
- Crayons or paints

Chapter 20: The Proof Is in the Fruit
- Nice, big delicious-looking apple
- Small, knotty apple
- Apple tree to be planted

Chapter 21: Your Favorite Shirt Color
- Variety of different-colored shirts and/or blouses
- T-shirts to be decorated

Chapter 22: God's Stamp of Approval
- Rubber name stamp and inkpad
- Rubber stamps (butterflies?) and inkpads for children

Chapter 23: My Name Is David
- Picture or small statue of a shepherd boy
- Shepherd's clothing and staff (for dramatic purposes)

Chapter 24: Little But Large
- Digital camera card
- Printer and paper to print pictures

Chapter 25: Are We Ever Alone?
✋ Globe

Chapter 26: No Vacation for God
✋ Toys appropriate to vacation time (beach ball, beach mat, camping gear, etc.)

About the Author

Randy Hammer

Randy Hammer has over thirty years of experience in pastoral ministry. He has worked with children in Vacation Church School, outdoor ministry, and of course, during the children's sermon time. His number one passion in ministry has been the preparation and delivery of sermons. Other passions include writing poetry and devotional materials, woodworking, and spending time with his wife, children, and their grandchildren.

He is the author of *Dancing in the Dark: Lessons in Facing Life's Challenges with Courage and Creativity* (1999, The Pilgrim Press), *Everyone a Butterfly: Forty Sermons for Children* (2004, Skinner House), *The Talking Stick: 40 Children's Sermons with Activities* (2007, The Pilgrim Press), *52 Ways to Ignite Your Congregation . . .Practical Hospitality* (2009, The Pilgrim Press) and *The Singing Bowl: 26 Children's Sermons with Activities* (2009, The Pilgrim Press).

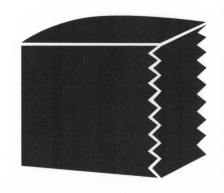

TASTE THE BREAD
30 Children's Sermons on Communion

Phyllis Vos Wezeman, Anna L. Liechty,
and Kenneth R. Wezeman

ISBN 0-8298-1519-8
paper/96 pages/$10.00

TOUCH THE WATER
30 Children's Sermons on Baptism

Phyllis Vos Wezeman, Anna L. Liechty,
and Kenneth R. Wezeman

ISBN 0-8298-1518-X
112 pages/paper/$10.00

PLANTINGS SEEDS OF FAITH

Virginia H. Loewen

ISBN 0-8298-1473-6
96 pages/paper/$10.00

GROWING SEEDS OF FAITH

Virginia H. Loewen

ISBN 0-8298-1488-4
96 pages/paper/$10.00

THE BROWN BAG

Jerry Marshall Jordan

ISBN 0-8298-0411-0
117 pages/paper/$9.95

SMALL WONDERS
Sermons for Children

Glen E. Rainsley

ISBN 0-8298-1252-0
104 pages/paper/$12.95

TIME WITH OUR CHILDREN
Stories for Use in Worship, Year B

Dianne E. Deming

ISBN 0-8298-0952-X
182 pages/paper/$9.95

TIME WITH OUR CHILDREN
Stories for Use in Worship, Year C

Dianne E. Deming

ISBN 0-8298-0953-8
157 pages/paper/$9.95

To order these or any other books from The Pilgrim Press call or write to:

The Pilgrim Press
700 Prospect Avenue East
Cleveland, Ohio 44115-1100

Phone orders: 1-800-537-3394 • Fax orders: 216-736-2206
Please include shipping charges of $6.00 for the first book and
$1.00 for each additional book.
Or order from our web sites at
www.pilgrimpress.com and www.ucpress.com.

Prices subject to change without notice.